H.G. Wells' FLOOR GAMES:

A Father's Account of Play and Its Legacy of Healing

Barbara A. Turner, Ph.D.
Editor

H.G. Wells' *Floor Games*: A Father's Account of Play and its Legacy of Healing

Floor Games, written by H.G. Wells and illustrated by J.R. Sinclair, was originally published by Frank Palmer 12-14 Red Lion Court, London in 1911. The work is reprinted here in its entirety, with enhancements to the original drawings by Charlotte M. Turner, PhD.

Photographs of Wells as a boy, Wells and Jane on their bicycle and the Wells children as infants, as well as the *picshua* illustration of daily life in the Wells household are from H.G. Wells' *Experiment in Autobiography: Discoveries and Conclusions of a Very Ordinary Brain (Since 1866)*, copyright 1934 by H.G. Wells, published by The Macmillan Company, New York. They are reprinted here by permission of A.P. Watt Ltd. on behalf of the Literary Executors of the Estate of H.G. Wells.

Published by
TEMENOS PRESS®, Box 305, Cloverdale, California 95425
www.temenospress.com

1 2 3 4 5 6 7 8 9 10

ISBN 097285172-0

Edited and new material by Barbara A. Turner, PhD
Cover and book design by Charlotte M. Turner, PhD

Printed in the United States of America.

Library of Congress Cataloging in Publications Data

Wells, H.G. (Herbert George), 1866-1946
[Floor Games]
H.G. Wells' Floor Games: a father's account of play and its legacy of healing / Barbara A. Turner, editor.
p. cm.
SUMMARY: Suggests some of the games that can be created using toy soldiers and other figurines, blocks, boards and planks, and toy trains arranged in various ways on an appropriate floor. New postscript offers biographical sketches of Wells, Margaret Lowenfeld, and Dora M. Kalff, and describes how Wells' book inspired the development of sandplay therapy.
LCCN 2004090234
ISBN 097285172-0

1. Games—Juvenile literature. 2. Wells, H.G. (Herbert George), 1866-1946. 3. Sandplay—Therapeutic use. 4. Games. I. Turner, Barbara A. II. Title.

GV1203.W6 2004 793'.019'22
QBI04-200250

Contents

Prolog

Temenos Press is pleased to return the timeless wisdom of *Floor Games* to print, along with a Postscript explaining its impact on child psychotherapy.

H.G. Wells penned *Floor Games* in 1911 as an account of his sons'[1] play with miniature worlds. Wells had a deep appreciation for the transformative powers of play and wanted to share it with others. Long out of print and in the public domain, *Floor Games* is reproduced here in its entirety, complete with original photographs, as well as marginal drawings enhanced and restored from J.R. Sinclair's original illustrations.

At the time *Floor Games* was written, it was eclipsed by Wells' voluminous other writings. *Floor Games* receded into the shadows of obscurity and may have been forgotten entirely, were it not for a singular reader who had a deep passion for the well-being of children, British pediatrician, Dr. Margaret Lowenfeld. *Floor Games* would eventually inspire Lowenfeld's renowned child treatment modality known as the *World Technique*. In turn, the World Technique would inspire the *sandplay method* of Swiss Jungian therapist, Dora M. Kalff. Today, these powerful psychotherapeutic techniques are used around the globe for treatment of both children and adults. We will discuss these matters later, in our Postscript.

But first, however, let's PLAY...

[1]Within the text of *Floor Games*, Wells refers to his sons by their initials: F.R.W. (Frank R. Wells) and G.P.W. (G.P. "Gip" Wells). He refers to himself as H.G.W.

A general view of the wonderful islands, showing Captain F.R.W's ship at anchor.

FLOOR GAMES

by

H.G. WELLS

Original Marginal Drawings by

J.R. Sinclair

Restored/Enhanced by C.M. Turner, Ph.D.

FLOOR GAMES By H.G. Wells

Section I

THE TOYS TO HAVE

FLOOR GAMES by H.G. Wells

THE TOYS TO HAVE

The jolliest indoor games for boys and girls demand a floor, and the home that has no floor upon which games may be played falls so far short of happiness. It must be a floor covered with linoleum or cork carpet, so that toy soldiers and such-like will stand up upon it, and of a colour and surface that will take and show chalk marks; the common green-coloured cork carpet without a pattern is the best of all. It must be no highway to

other rooms, and well lit and airy. Occasionally, alas! it must be scrubbed—and then a truce to Floor Games. Upon such a floor may be made an infinitude of imaginative games, not only keeping boys and girls happy for days together, but building up a framework of spacious and inspiring ideas in them for after life. The British Empire will gain new strength from nursery floors. I am going to tell of some of these games and what is most needed to play them; I have tried them all and a score of others like them with my sons, and all of the games here illustrated have been set out by us. I am going to tell of them here because I think what we have done will interest other fathers and mothers, and perhaps be of use to them (and to uncles and such-like tributary sub-species of humanity)

in buying presents for their own and other people's children.

Now, the toys we play with time after time, and in a thousand permutations and combinations, belong to four main groups. We have:

(1) SOLDIERS, and with these I class sailors, railway porters, civilians, and the lower animals generally, such as I will presently describe in greater detail;

(2) BRICKS;

(3) BOARDS and PLANKS;

and

(4) a lot of CLOCKWORK RAILWAY ROLLING STOCK and RAILS.

Also there are certain minor objects—tin ships, Easter eggs, and the like—of which I shall make incidental mention, that like the kiwi

and the duck-billed platypus refuse to be classified. These we arrange and rearrange in various ways upon our floor, making a world of them. In doing so we have found out all sorts of pleasant facts, and also many undesirable possibilities; and very probably our experience will help a reader here and there to the former and save him from the latter.

For instance, our planks and boards, and what one can do with them, have been a great discovery. Lots of boys and girls seem to be quite without planks and boards at all, and there is no regular trade in them. The toyshops did not keep anything of the sort. (We don't, as a matter of fact, think very much of toyshops. We think

they trifle with great possibilities. We consider them expensive and incompetent, and flatten our noses against their plate glass perhaps, but only in the most critical spirit.) Our boards, which we had to get made by a carpenter, are the basis of half the games we play. The planks and boards we have are of various sizes. We began with three of two yards by one; they were made with cross pieces like small doors; but these we found unnecessarily large, and we would not get them now after our present experience. The best thickness, we think, is an inch for the larger sizes and three-quarters and a half inch for the smaller; and the best

sizes are a yard square, thirty inches square, two feet, and eighteen inches square--one or two of each, and a greater number of smaller ones, 18 x 9, 9 x 9, and 9 x 4-1/2. With the larger ones we make islands and archipelagos on our floor while the floor is a sea, or we make a large island or a couple on the Venice pattern, or we pile the smaller on the larger to make hills when the floor is a level plain, or they roof in railway stations or serve as bridges, in such manner as I will presently illustrate. And these boards of ours pass into our next most important possession, which is our box of bricks.

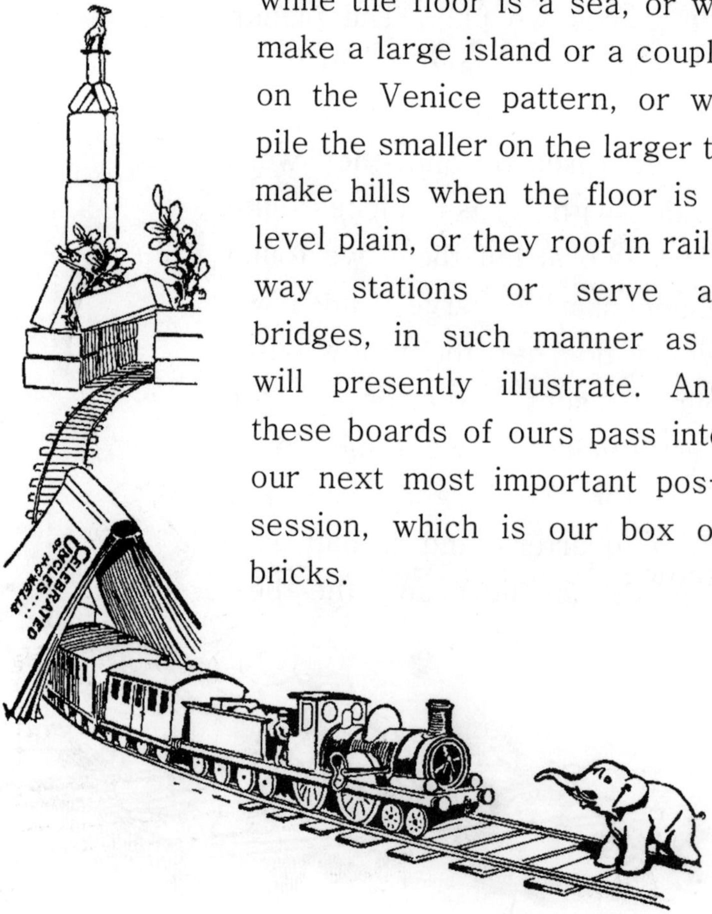

(But I was nearly forgetting to tell this, that all the thicker and larger of these boards have holes bored through them. At about every four inches is a hole, a little larger than an ordinary gimlet hole. These holes have their uses, as I will tell later, but now let me get on to the box of bricks.)

This, again, wasn't a toyshop acquisition. It came to us by gift from two generous friends, unhappily growing up and very tall at that; and they had it from parents who were one of several families who shared in the benefit of a Good Uncle. I know nothing certainly of this

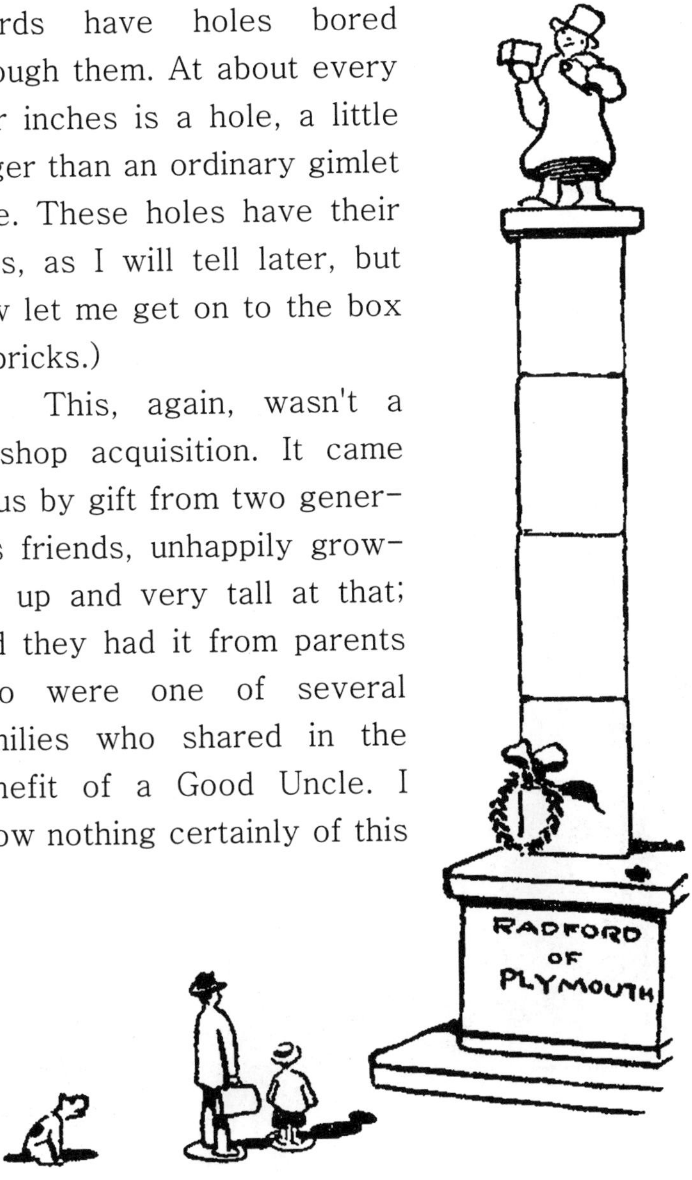

man except that he was a Radford of Plymouth. I have never learned nor cared to learn of his commoner occupations, but certainly he was one of those shining and distinguished uncles that tower up at times above the common levels of humanity. At times, when we consider our derived and undeserved share of his inheritance and count the joys it gives us, we have projected half in jest and half in earnest the putting together of a little exemplary book upon the subject of such exceptional men: *Celebrated Uncles*, it should be called; and it should stir up all who read it to some striving at least towards the glories of

A view showing the Island of the Temple and the invasion of the Red Indians' territory by Captain G.P.W.

the avuncular crown. What this great benefactor did was to engage a deserving unemployed carpenter through an entire winter making big boxes of wooden bricks for the almost innumerable nephews and nieces with which an appreciative circle of brothers and sisters had blessed him. There are whole bricks 4-1/2 inches x 2-1/4 x 1-1/8; and there are quarters--called by those previous owners (who have now ascended to, we hope but scarcely believe, a happier life near the ceiling) "piggys." You note how these sizes fit into the sizes of the boards, and of each size--we have never counted them, but we must have hundreds. We can pave a dozen square yards of floor with them.

How utterly we despise the silly little bricks of the toy-shops! They are too small to make a decent home for even the poorest lead soldiers, even if there were hundreds of them, and there are never enough, never nearly enough; even if you take one at a time and lay it down and say, "This is a house," even then there are not enough. We see rich people, rich people out of motor cars, rich people beyond the dreams of avarice, going into toyshops and buying these skimpy, sickly, ridiculous pseudo-boxes of bricklets, because they do not know what to ask for, and the toyshops are just the merciless mercenary ene-mies of youth and happiness --

so far, that is, as bricks are concerned. Their unfortunate under-parented offspring mess about with these gifts, and don't make very much of them, and put them away; and you see their consequences in after life in the weakly-conceived villas and silly suburbs that people have built all round London. Such poor under-nourished nurseries must needs fall back upon the *Encyclopedia Britannica,* and even that is becoming flexible on India paper! But our box of bricks almost satisfies. With our box of bricks we can scheme and build, all three of us, for the best part of the hour, and still have more bricks in the box.

So much now for the bricks. I will tell later how we

use cartridge paper and card and other things to help in our building, and of the decorative use we make of plasticine. Of course, it goes without saying that we despise those foolish, expensive, made-up wooden and pasteboard castles that are sold in shops--playing with them is like playing with somebody else's dead game in a state of *rigor mortis*.

Let me now say a little about toy soldiers and the world to which they belong. Toy soldiers used to be flat, small creatures in my own boyhood, in comparison with the magnificent beings one can buy today. There has been an enormous improvement in our national physique in this respect. Now they stand nearly two inches

high and look you broadly in the face, and they have the movable arms and alert intelligence of scientifically exercised men. You get five of them mounted or nine afoot in a box for tenpence halfpenny. We three like those of British manufacture best; other makes are of incompatible sizes, and we have a rule that saves much trouble, that all red coats belong to G.P.W., and all other coloured coats to F.R.W., all gifts, bequests, and accidents notwithstanding. Also we have sailors; but, since there are no red-coated sailors, blue counts as red.

Then we have beefeaters. Red Indians, Zulus, for whom there are special rules. We find we can buy lead dogs, cats, lions, tigers, horses, camels, cattle, and ele-

phants of a reasonably corresponding size, and we have also several boxes of railway porters, and some soldiers we bought in Hesse-Darmstadt that we pass off on an unsuspecting home world as policemen. But we want civilians very badly. We found a box of German civilians once in a shop in Oxford Street, near the Marble Arch, the right size but rather heavy, and running to nearly twopence halfpenny apiece (which is too dear), gentlemen in tweed suits carrying bags, a top-hatted gentleman, ladies in grey and white, two children, and a dog, and so on, but we have never been able to find any more. They do not seem

to be made in England at all--will toy manufacturers please note? I write now as if I were British Consul General in Toyland, noting new opportunities for trade. Consequent upon this dearth, our little world suffers from an exaggerated curse of militarism, and even the grocer wears epaulettes. This might please Lord Roberts and Mr. Leo Maxse, but it certainly does not please us. I wish, indeed, that we could buy boxes of tradesmen: a blue butcher, a white baker with a loaf of standard bread, a draper or so; boxes of servants, boxes of street traffic, smart sets, and so forth. We could do with a judge and barristers, or a box of ves-

trymen. It is true that we can buy Salvation Army lasses and football players, but we are cold to both of these. We have, of course, boy scouts. With such boxes of civilians we could have much more fun than with the running, marching, swashbuckling soldiery that pervades us. They drive us to reviews; and it is only emperors, kings, and very silly small boys who can take an undying interest in uniforms and reviews.

And lastly, of our railways, let me merely remark here that we have always insisted upon one uniform gauge. We have adhered rigidly to gauge *O*, and everything we buy fits into and develops our

existing railway system. Nothing is more indicative of the wambling sort of parent and a coterie of witless, worthless uncles than a heap of railway toys of different gauges and natures in the children's playroom.

And so, having told you of the material we have, let me now tell you of one or two games (out of the innumerable many) that we have played. Of course, in this I have to be a little artificial. Actual games of the kind I am illustrating here have been played by us, many and many a time, with joy and happy invention and no thought of publication. They have gone now, those games, into that vaguely luminous and iridescent world of memories into which all love-engendering happiness must go. But we have tried our best to set them out again and recall the good points in them here.

A close view of the temple, whose portals are guarded by grotesque plasticine monsters.

FLOOR GAMES by H.G. Wells

Section II

THE GAME OF THE WONDERFUL ISLANDS

FLOOR GAMES by H.G. Wells

THE GAME OF THE WONDERFUL ISLANDS

In this game the floor is the sea. Half--rather the larger half because of some instinctive right of primogeniture--is assigned to the elder of my two sons (he is, as it were, its Olympian), and the other half goes to his brother. We distribute our boards about the sea in an archipelagic manner. We then dress our islands, objecting strongly to too close a scrutiny of our proceed-

ings until we have done. Here, in the illustration, is such an archipelago ready for its explorers, or rather on the verge of exploration. On the whole it is Indian in character--comprehensively Indian, east and west and Red Indian, as befits children of an imperial people. There are altogether four islands, two to the reader's right and two to the left, and the nearer ones are the more northerly; it is as many as we could get into the camera. The northern island to the right is most advanced in civilisation, and is chiefly temple. That temple has a flat roof, diversified by domes made of half Easter eggs and those card things the cream cones come in. These are surmounted by decorative work of a flamboyant character in plas-

ticine, designed by G.P.W. An oriental population crowds the courtyard and pours out upon the roadway. Note the grotesque plasticine monsters who guard the portals, also by G.P.W., who had a free hand with the architecture of this remarkable specimen of eastern religiosity. They are nothing, you may be sure, to the gigantic idols inside, out of the reach of the sacrilegious camera. To the right is a tropical thatched hut. The thatched roof is really that nice ribbed paper that comes round bottles--a priceless boon to these games. All that comes into the house is saved for us. The owner of the hut lounges outside the door. He is a dismounted cavalry-

corps man, and he owns one cow. It cost ninepence half-penny--a monstrous sum. If the toy soldier manufacturers had the sense to sell boxes of cows and pigs, his farm, poor dear, would be better stocked. But

they haven't; they just go on making soldiers. His fence, I may note, belonged to a little wooden farm we bought in Switzerland. Its human inhabitants are scattered; its beasts follow a precarious living as wild guinea-pigs on the islands to the south.

Your attention is particularly directed to the trees about and behind the temple, which thicken to a forest on the further island to the right. These trees we make of twigs taken from trees and bushes in the garden, and stuck into holes in our

boards. Formerly we lived in a house with a little wood close by, and our forests were wonderful. Now we are restricted to a Hampstead garden, and we could get nothing for this set out but jasmine and pear. Both have wilted a little, and are not nearly such spirited trees as you can make out of tamarisk, euonymus, fir, ilex, or may. It is for these woods chiefly that we have our planks perforated with little holes. No tin trees can ever be so plausible and various and jolly as these. With a good garden to draw upon one can make terrific sombre woods, and then lie down and look through them at lonely horsemen or wandering beasts.

That further island on the right is a less settled country than the island of the temple. Camels, you note, run wild there; there is a sort of dwarf elephant, similar to the

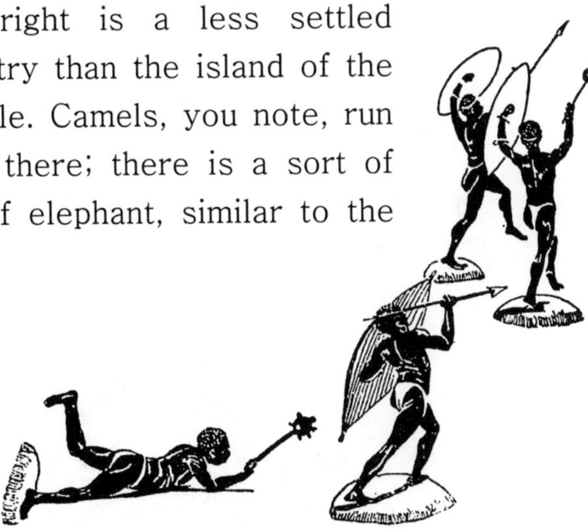

now extinct kind of which one finds skeletons in Malta, pigs (or rather--confound those unenterprising tradesmen! -- one costly inadequate pig), a red parrot, and other such creatures, of lead and wood. The pear-trees are fine. It is those which have attracted white settlers (I suppose they are), whose thatched huts are to be seen both upon the beach and inland. By the huts on the beach lie a number of pear-tree logs; but a raid of negroid savages from the adjacent island to the left is in progress, and the only settler clearly visible is the man in a rifleman's uniform running inland for help. Beyond, peeping out among the trees, are the supports he seeks.

These same negroid savages are as bold as they are fero-

A view showing the raid of the Negroid savages upon the White settlers of Pear Tree Island.

cious. They cross arms of the sea upon their rude canoes, made simply of a strip of cardboard. Their own island, the one to the south-left, is a rocky wilderness containing caves. Their chief food is the wild-goat, but in pursuit of these creatures you will also sometimes find the brown sixpenny bear, who sits--he is small but perceptible to the careful student--in the mouth of his cave. Here, too, you will distinguish small guinea-pig-like creatures of wood, in happier days the inhabitants of that Swiss farm. Sunken rocks off this island are indicated by a white foam which takes the form of letters, and you will also note a whirlpool between the two islands to the right.

Finally comes the island nearest to the reader on the left. This also is wild and rocky, inhabited not by negroid blacks, but by Red Indians, whose tents, made by F.R.W. out of ordinary brown paper and adorned with chalk totems of a rude and characteristic kind, pour forth their fierce and well-armed inhabitants at the intimation of an invader. The rocks on this island, let me remark, have great mineral wealth. Among them are to be found not only sheets and veins of silver paper, but great nuggets of metal, obtained by the melting down of hopelessly broken soldiers in an iron spoon. Note, too, the peculiar and romantic shell beach of this coun-

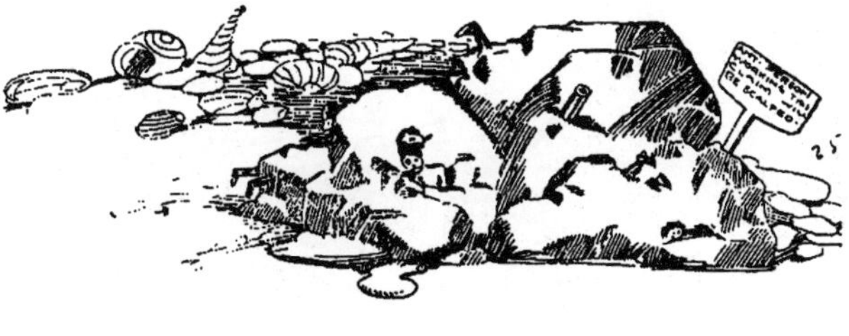

try. It is an island of exceptional interest to the geologist and scientific explorer. The Indians, you observe, have domesticated one leaden and one wooden cow (see remarks above on the dearth of lead animals).

This is how the game would be set out. Then we build ships and explore these islands, but in these pictures the ships are represented as already arriving. The ships are built out of our wooden bricks on flat keels made of two wooden pieces of 9 x 4-1/2 inches, which are very convenient to push about over the floor. Captain G.P.W. is steaming into the bight between the eastern and western islands. He carries heavy guns, his ship bristles with an ex-

tremely aggressive soldiery, who appear to be blazing away for the mere love of the thing. (I suspect him of Imperialist intentions.) Captain F.R.W. is apparently at anchor between his northern and southern islands. His ship is of a slightly more pacific type. I note on his deck a lady and a gentleman (of German origin) with a bag, two of our all too rare civilians. No doubt the bag contains samples and a small conversation dictionary in the negroid dialects. (I think F.R.W. may turn out to be a Liberal.) Perhaps he will sail on and rescue the raided huts, perhaps he will land and build a jetty, and begin mining among the rocks to fill his hold with silver. Perhaps the natives

will kill and eat the gentleman with the bag. All that is for Captain F.R.W. to decide.

You see how the game goes on. We land and alter things, and build and rearrange, and hoist paper flags on pins, and subjugate populations, and confer all the blessings of civilization upon these lands. We keep them going for days. And at last, as we begin to tire of them, comes the scrubbing brush, and we must burn our trees and dismantle our islands, and put our soldiers in the little nests of drawers, and stand the island boards up against the wall, and put everything away. Then perhaps, after a few days, we begin upon some other such game, just as we feel disposed. But it is never quite the same game, never. Another time it may be wildernesses for example, and the boards

Some suggestions for toy makers.

are hills, and never a drop of water is to be found except for the lakes and rivers we may mark out in chalk. But after one example others are easy, and next I will tell you of our way of making towns.

FLOOR GAMES by H.G. Wells

Section III

OF THE BUILDING OF CITIES

A general view of Chamois City, showing the Cherry Tree Inn and the shopping quarter.

OF THE BUILDING OF CITIES

We always build twin cities, like London and Westminster, or Buda-Pesth, because two of us always want, both of them, to be lord mayors and municipal councils, and it makes for local freedom and happiness to arrange

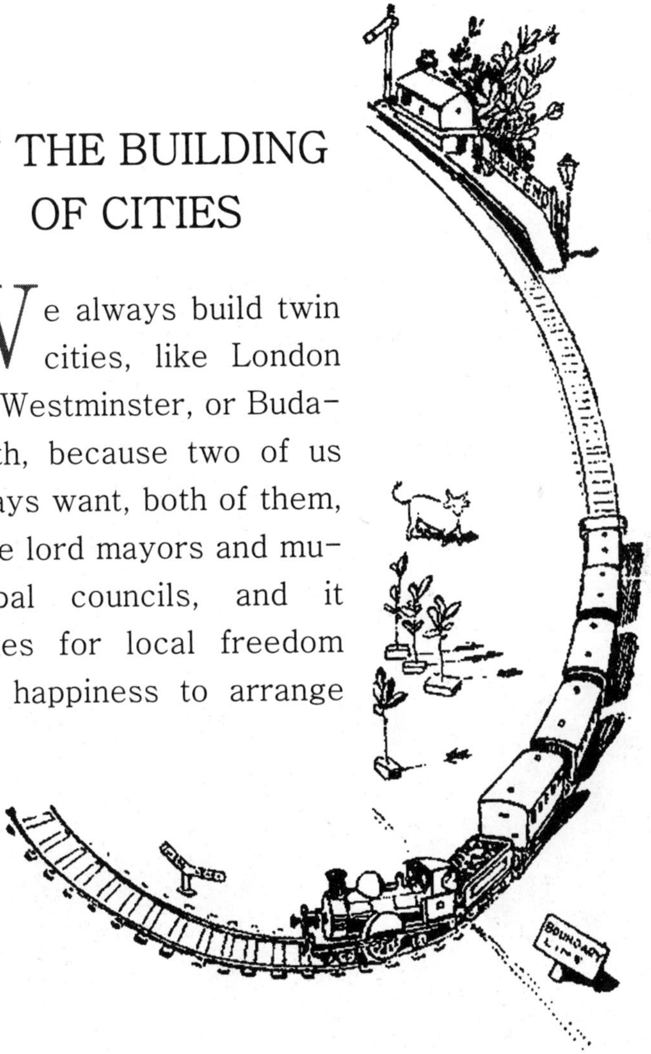

it so; but when railways or tramways are involved we have our rails in common, and we have an excellent law that rails must be laid down and points kept open in such a manner that anyone feeling so disposed may send a through train from their own station back to their own station again without needless negotiation or the personal invasion of anybody else's administrative area. It is an undesirable thing to have other people bulging over one's houses, standing in one's open spaces, and, in extreme cases, knocking down and even treading on one's citizens. It leads at times to explanations that are afterwards regretted.

We always have twin cities, or at the utmost stage of coalescence a city with two wards, Red End and Blue End; we mark the boundaries very carefully, and our citizens have so much local patriotism (Mr. Chesterton will learn with pleasure) that they stray but rarely over that thin little streak of white that bounds their municipal allegiance. Sometimes we have an election for mayor; it is like a census but very abusive, and Red always wins. Only citizens with two legs and at least one arm and capable of standing up may vote, and voters may poll on

horseback; boy scouts and women and children do not vote, though there is a vigorous agitation to remove these disabilities. Zulus and foreign- looking persons, such as Indian cavalry and Red Indians, are also disfranchised. So are riderless horses and camels; but the elephant has never attempted to vote on any occasion, and does not seem to desire the privilege. It influences public opinion quite sufficiently as it is by nodding its head.

We have set out and I have photographed one of our cities to illustrate more clearly the amusement of the game. Red End is to the reader's right, and includes most of the hill on which the town stands, a shady zoological garden, the town hall, a railway tunnel through the hill, a museum (away in the extreme right-hand corner), a church,

a rifle range, and a shop. Blue End has the railway station, four or five shops, several homes, a public-house, and a thatched farm cottage, close to the railway station. The boundary drawn by me as overlord (who also made the hills and tunnels and appointed the trees to grow) runs irregularly between the two shops nearest the cathedral, over the shoulder in front of the town hall, and between the thatched farm and the rifle range.

The nature of the hills I have already explained, and this time we have had no lakes or ornamental water. These are very easily made out of a piece of glass--the glass lid of a box for

example--laid upon silver paper. Such water becomes very readily populated by those celluloid seals and swans and ducks that are now so common. Paper fish appear below the surface and may be peered at by the curious. But on this occasion we have nothing of the kind, nor have we made use of a green-coloured tablecloth we sometimes use to drape our hills. Of course, a large part of the fun of this game lies in the witty incorporation of all sorts of extraneous objects. But the incorporation must be witty, or you may soon convert the whole thing into an incoherent muddle-heap of half-good ideas.

I have taken two photographs, one to the right and one to the left of this agreeable

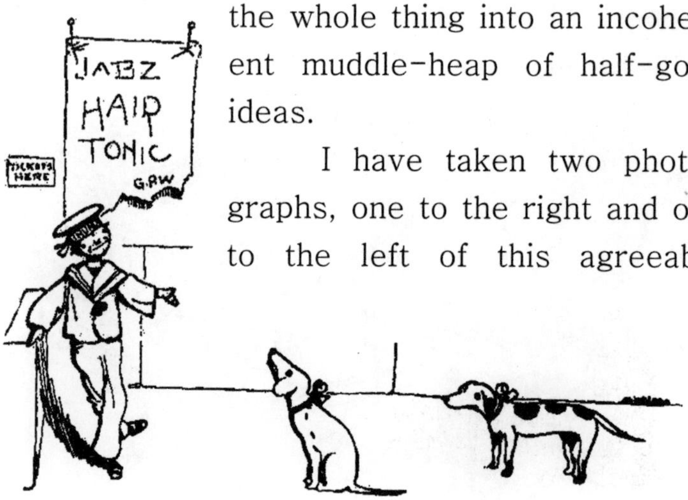

place. I may perhaps adopt a kind of guide-book style in reviewing its principal features: I begin at the railway station. I have made a rather nearer and larger photograph of the railway station, which presents a diversified and entertaining scene to the incoming visitor. Porters (out of a box of porters) career here and there with the trucks and light luggage. Quite a number of our all-too-rare civilians parade the platform: two gentlemen, a lady, and a small but evil-looking child are particularly noticeable; and there is a penny wooden sailor with jointed legs, in a state of intoxication as reprehensible as it is nowadays happily rare. Two virtuous dogs regard his abandon with quiet scorn. The seat on which he sprawls is a

broken piece of some toy whose nature I have long forgotten, the station clock is a similar fragment, and so is the metallic pillar which bears the name of the station. So many toys, we find, only become serviceable with a little smashing. There is an allegory in this--as Hawthorne used to write in his diary.

What is he doing, the great god Pan,
Down in the reeds by the river?

The fences at the ends of the platforms are pieces of wood belonging to the game of Matador--that splendid and very educational construction game, hailing, I believe, from Hungary, which is slowly but

The railway station at Blue End.

surely making its way to the affections of English children. There is also, I regret to say, a blatant advertisement of Jab's "Hair Colour," showing the hair. (In the photograph the hair does not come out very plainly.) This is by G.P.W., who seems marked out by destiny to be the advertisement-writer of the next generation. He spends much of his scanty leisure inventing and drawing advertisements of imaginary commodities. Oblivious to many happy, beautiful, and noble things in life, he goes about studying and imitating the literature of the hoardings and tubelifts. He and his brother write newspapers almost entirely devoted to these annoying appeals. You will note, too, the placard at the mouth of the rail-

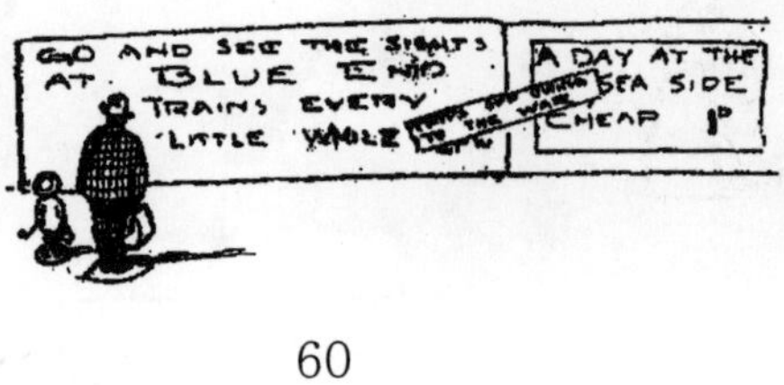

way tunnel urging the existence of Jinks' Soap upon the passing traveller. The oblong object on the placard represents, no doubt, a cake of this offensive and aggressive commodity. The zoological garden flaunts a placard, "Zoo, Id. pay," and the grocer's picture of a cabbage with "Get Them" is not to be ignored. F.R.W. is more like the London County Council in this respect, and prefers bare walls. You will, I hope, be able to read his notice on the inn: "£5, who sticks bills here."

"Returning from the station," as the guide-books say, and "giving one more glance" at the passengers who are waiting for the privilege of going round the circle in open trucks and returning in a prostrated condition to the

station again, and "observing" what admirable platforms are made by our 9 x 4-1/2 pieces, we pass out to the left into the village street. A motor omnibus (a one-horse hospital cart in less progressive days) stands waiting for passengers; and, on our way to the Cherry Tree Public-House, we remark two nurses, one in charge of a child with a plasticine head. The landlord of the inn is a small grotesque figure of plaster; his sign is fastened on by a pin. No doubt the refreshment supplied here has an enviable reputation, to judge by the alacrity with

which a number of riflemen move towards the door. The inn, by the by, like the station and some private houses, is roofed with stiff paper.

These stiff-paper roofs are one of our great inventions. We get thick, stiff paper at twopence a sheet and cut it to the sizes we need. After the game is over, we put these roofs inside one another and stick them into the bookshelves. The roof one folds and puts away will live to roof another day.

Proceeding on our way past the Cherry Tree, and resisting cosy invitation of its portals, we come to the shopping quarter of the town. The stock in windows is

made by hand out of plasticine. We note the meat and hams of "Mr. Woddy," the cabbages and carrots of "Tod & Brothers," the general activities of the "Jokil Co." shopmen. It is *de rigueur* with our shop assistants that they should wear white helmets. In the street, boy scouts go to and fro, a waggon clatters by; most of the adult population is about its business, and a red-coated band plays along the roadway. Contrast this animated scene with the mysteries of sea and forest, rock and whirlpool, in our previous game. Further on is the big church or cathedral. It is built in an extremely debased Gothic style; it reminds us most of a church we once sur-

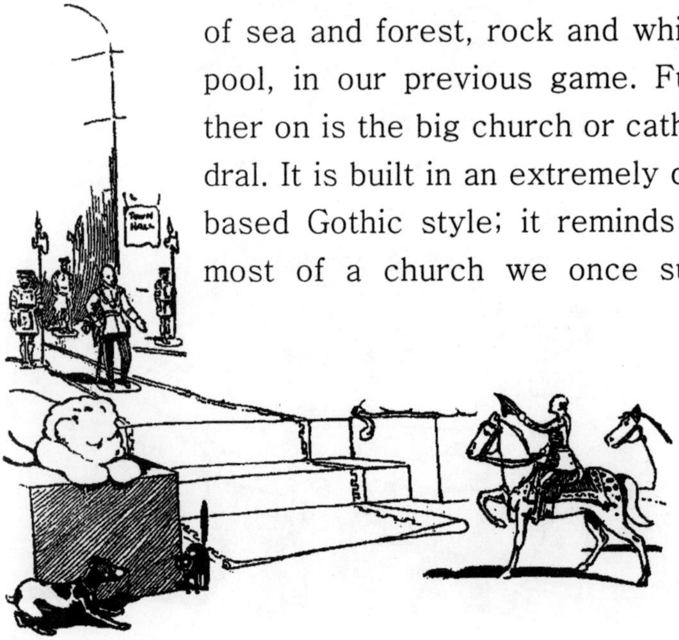

veyed during a brief visit to Rotterdam on our way up the Rhine. A solitary boy scout, mindful of the views of Lord Haldane, enters its high portal. Passing the cathedral, we continue to the museum. This museum is no empty boast; it contains mineral specimens, shells--such great shells as were found on the beaches of our previous game--the Titanic skulls of extinct rabbits and cats, and other such wonders. The slender curious may lie down on the floor and peep in at the windows.

"We now," says the guide-book, "retrace our steps to the shops, and then, turning to the left, ascend under the trees up the terraced hill on which stands the Town

Hall. This magnificent building is surmounted by a colossal statue of a chamois, the work of a Wengen artist; it is in two stories, with a battlemented roof, and a crypt (entrance to right of steps) used for the incarceration of offenders. It is occupied by the town guard, who wear beefeater costumes of ancient origin."

Note the red parrot perched on the battlements; it lives tame in the zoological gardens, and is of the same species as one we formerly observed in our archipelago. Note, too, the brisk cat-and-dog encounter below. Steps descend in wide flights down the hillside into Blue End. The two couchant lions on either side of the steps are in

plasticine, and were executed by that versatile artist, who is also mayor of Red End, G.P.W. He is present. Our photographer has hit upon a happy moment in the history of this town, and a conversation of the two mayors is going on upon the terrace before the palace. F.R.W., mayor of Blue End, stands on the steps in the costume of a British admiral; G.P.W. is on horseback (his habits are equestrian) on the terrace. The town guard parades in their honour, and up the hill a number of blue-clad musicians (a little hidden by trees) ride on gray horses towards them.

Passing in front of the town hall, and turning to the

The terraced hill on which stands the town hall. Behind can be seen the zoological gardens.

right, we approach the zoological gardens. Here we pass two of our civilians: a gentleman in black, a lady, and a large boy scout, presumably their son. We enter the gardens, which are protected by a bearded janitor, and remark at once a band of three performing dogs, who are, as the guide-book would say, "discoursing sweet music." In neither ward of the city does there seem to be the slightest restraint upon the use of musical instruments. It is no place for neurotic people.

The gardens contain the inevitable elephants, camels (which we breed, and which are therefore in considerable numbers), a sitting bear, brought from last game's caves, goats from the same region, tamed and now running loose

in the gardens, dwarf elephants, wooden nondescripts, and other rare creatures. The keepers wear a uniform not unlike that of railway guards and porters. We wander through the gardens, return, descend the hill by the school of musketry, where soldiers are to be seen shooting at the butts, pass through the paddock of the old thatched farm, and so return to the railway station, extremely gratified by all we have seen, and almost equally divided in our minds between the merits and attractiveness of either ward. A clockwork train comes clattering into the station, we take our places, somebody hoots or whistles for the engine (which can't), the signal is knocked over in the excitement of the moment, the

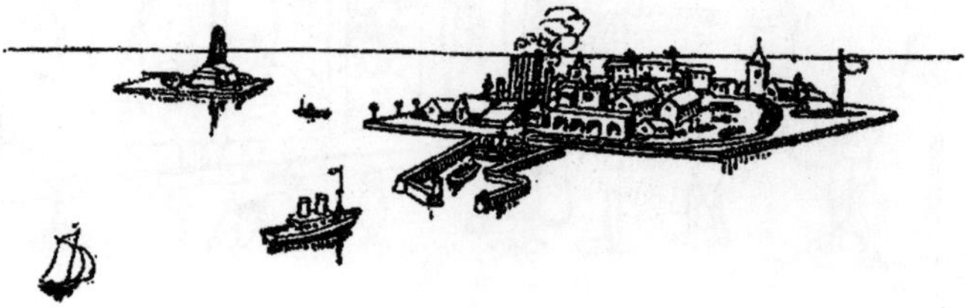

train starts, and we "wave a long, regretful farewell to the salubrious cheerfulness of Chamois City."

You see now how we set out and the spirit in which we set out our towns. It demands but the slightest exercise of the imagination to devise a hundred additions and variations of the scheme. You can make picture-galleries--great fun for small boys who can draw; you can make factories; you can plan out flower-gardens--which appeals very strongly to intelligent little girls; your town hall may become a fortified castle; or you may put the whole town on boards and make a Venice of it, with ships and boats upon its canals, and bridges across them. We used to

have some very serviceable ships of cardboard, with flat bottoms; and then we used to have a harbor, and the ships used to sail away to distant rooms, and even into the garden, and return with the most remarkable cargoes, loads of nasturtium-stem logs, for example. We had sacks then, made of glove-fingers, and several toy cranes. I suppose we could find most of these again if we hunted for them. Once, with this game fresh in our minds we went to see the docks, which struck us as just our old harbor game magnified.

"I say, Daddy," said one of us in a quiet corner, wistfully, as one who speaks knowingly against the probabilities of the case, and yet with a faint, thin hope,

"couldn't we play just for a little with these sacks . . . until somebody comes?"

Of course the setting-out of the city is half the game. Then you devise incidents. As I wanted to photograph the particular set-out for the purpose of illustrating this account, I took a larger share in the arrangement than I usually do. It was necessary to get everything into the picture, to ensure a light background that would throw up some of the trees, prevent too much overlapping, and things like that. When the photographing was over, matters became more normal. I left the schoolroom, and when I returned I found that the group of riflemen which had been converging on the public-house had been sharply recalled to duty, and were

trotting in a disciplined, cheerless way towards the railway station. The elephant had escaped from the zoo into the Blue Ward, and was being marched along by a military patrol. The originally scattered boy scouts were being paraded. G. P. W. had demolished the shop of the Jokil Company, and was building a Red End station near the bend. The stock of the Jokil Company had passed into the hands of the adjacent storekeepers. Then the town hall ceremonies came to an end and the guard marched off. Then G. P. W. demolished the rifle-range, and ran a small branch of the urban railway uphill to the town hall door, and on into the zoological gardens. This was only the beginning of a period of enterprise in transit, a small railway boom. A number of halts of simple construction sprang up. There was much making of railway tickets, of a size that enabled passengers to stick their heads through the middle and wear them as a Mexi-

can does his blanket. Then a battery of artillery turned up in the High Street and there was talk of fortifications. Suppose wild Indians were to turn up across the plains to the left and attack the town! Fate still has toy drawers untouched.

So things will go on till putting-away night on Friday. Then we shall pick up the roofs and shove them away among the books, return the clockwork engines very carefully to their boxes, for engines are fragile things, stow the soldiers and civilians and animals in their nests of drawers, burn the trees again--this time they are sweet-bay; and all the joys and sorrows and rivalries and successes of Blue End and Red End will pass, and follow Carthage and Nineveh, the empire of Aztec and Roman, the arts of Eritrea and the palaces of Crete, and the plannings and contrivings of innumerable myriads of children, into the limbo of games exhausted . . . it may be, leaving some profit, in thoughts widened, in strengthened apprehensions; it may be, leaving nothing but a memory that dies.

FLOOR GAMES by H.G. Wells

Section IV
FUNICULARS, MARBLE TOWERS, CASTLES AND WAR GAMES, BUT VERY LITTLE OF WAR GAMES

FLOOR GAMES by H.G. Wells

FUNICULARS, MARBLE TOWERS, CASTLES AND WAR GAMES, BUT VERY LITTLE OF WAR GAMES

I have now given two general types of floor game; but these are only just two samples of delightful and imagination-stirring variations that can be contrived out of the toys I have described. I will now glance rather more shortly at some other very good

The school of musketry. On the terrace the town guard parades in honour of the two mayors.

uses of the floor, the boards, the bricks, the soldiers, and the railway system--that pentagram for exorcising the evil spirit of dulness from the lives of little boys and girls. And first, there is a kind of lark we call Funiculars. There are times when islands cease somehow to dazzle, and towns and cities are too orderly and uneventful and cramped for us, and we want something--something to whizz. Then we say: "Let us make a funicular. Let us make a funicular more than we have ever done. Let us make one to reach up to the table." We dispute whether it isn't a mountain railway we are after. The bare name is refreshing; it takes us back to that unforgettable time when we all went to

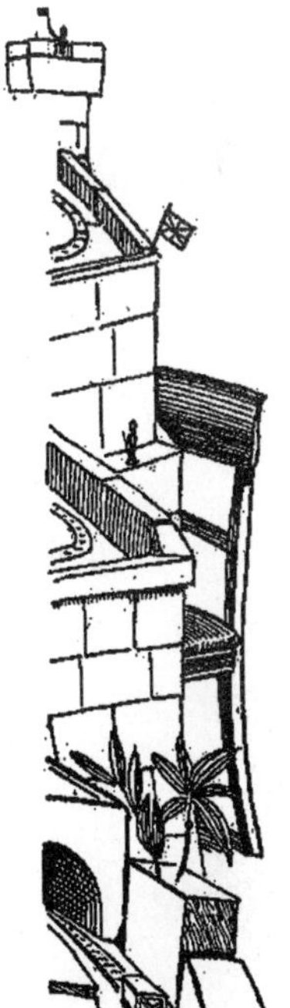

Wengen, winding in and out and up and up the mountain side--from slush, to such snow and sunlight as we had never seen before. And we make a mountain railway. So far, we have never got it up to the table, but some day we will. Then we will have a station there on the flat, and another station on the floor, with shunts and sidings to each.

The peculiar joy of the mountain railway is that, if it is properly made, a loaded truck -- not a toy engine; it is too rough a game for delicate, respectable engines -- will career from top to bottom of the system, and go this way and that as your cunningly-arranged points determine; and afterwards--and this is a wonderful and distinctive discovery--you

can send it back by 'lectric.

What is a 'lectric? You may well ask. 'Lectrics were invented almost by accident, by one of us, to whom also the name is due. It came out of an accident to a toy engine; a toy engine that seemed done for, and that was yet full of life.

You know, perhaps, what a toy engine is like. It has the general appearance of a railway engine; funnels, buffers, cab, and so forth. All these are very elegant things, no doubt; but they do not make for lightness, they do not facilitate hill-climbing. Now, sometimes an engine gets its clockwork out of order, and then it is over and done for; but sometimes it is merely the outer semblance that is injured -- the

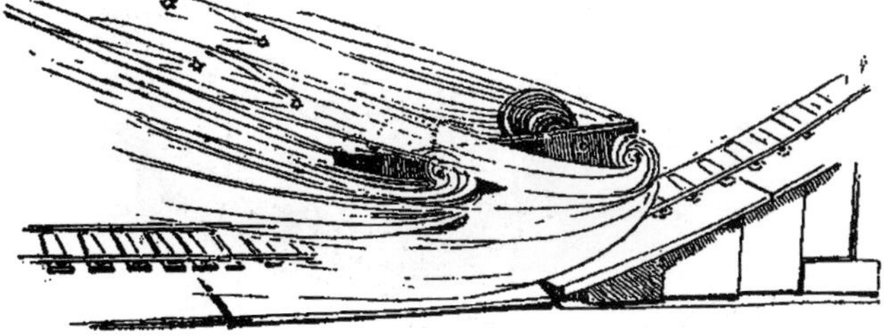

funnel bent, the body twisted. You remove the things and, behold! you have bare clockwork on wheels, an apparatus of almost malignant energy, soul without body, a kind of metallic rage. This it was that our junior member instantly knew for a 'lectric, and loved from the moment of its stripping.

(I have, by the by, known a very serviceable little road 'lectric made out of a clockwork mouse.)

Well, when we have got chairs and boxes and bricks, and graded our line skilfully and well, easing the descent, and being very careful of the joining at the bends for fear that the descending trucks and cars will jump the rails, we send down first an empty truck, then trucks loaded with bricks and

lead soldiers, and then the 'lectric; and then afterwards the sturdy 'lectric shoves up the trucks again to the top, with a kind of savagery of purpose and a whizz that is extremely gratifying to us. We make points in these lines; we make them have level-crossings, at which collisions are always being just averted; the lines go over and under each other, and in and out of tunnels.

The marble tower, again, is a great building, on which we devise devious slanting ways down which marbles run. I do not know why it is amusing to make a marble run down a long intricate path, and dollop down

steps, and come almost but not quite to a stop, and rush out of dark places and across little bridges of card: it is, and we often do it.

Castles are done with bricks and cardboard turrets and a portcullis of card, and drawbridge and moats; they are a mere special sort of city-building, done because we have a box of men in armor. We could reconstruct all sorts of historical periods if the toy soldier makers would provide us with people. But at present, as I have already complained, they make scarcely anything but contemporary fighting men. And of the war game I must either write volumes or nothing. For the present let it be nothing. Some day, perhaps, I will write a great book about the war game

and tell of battles and campaigns and strategy and tactics. But this time I set out merely to tell of the ordinary joys of playing with the floor, and to gird improvingly and usefully at toymakers. So much, I think, I have done. If one parent or one uncle buys the wiselier for me, I shall not altogether have lived in vain.

FLOOR GAMES by H.G. Wells

The End

Postscript

Hardly predictable at the time it was written, Wells' delightful account of the imaginative play of his own children evolved into an enduring field of child psychotherapy. *Floor Games* gave rise to Dr. Margaret Lowenfeld's World Technique, and subsequently, Jungian therapist Dora Kalff's Sandplay Method. To supplement the reader's appreciation of *Floor Games'* significance and impact, we present the following:

- **H.G. Wells: The Man Behind *Floor Games***. A sketch of the colorful life of H.G. Wells, touching upon the significant events in his personal life, as well as his background in play, all of which led to his creation of *Floor Games*,

- **Margaret Lowenfeld: Founder of the World Technique.** An account of *Floor Games'* influence on the life and work of Margaret Lowenfeld, resulting in the World Technique,

- **Dora Maria Kalff: Pioneer in Sandplay Therapy**. A description of Margaret Lowenfeld's influence on the work of Dora Kalff, leading to Kalff's renowned Sandplay Method,

- **The Sandplay Method**. A few specific details about the materials and techniques that comprise the Sandplay Method, and

- **Web Resources**. A list of websites from which the curious reader may obtain additional information about H.G. Wells, Margaret Lowenfeld, play therapy, and sandplay.

H.G. Wells

The Man Behind *Floor Games*

H.G. Wells was a fascinating man. He was a prolific writer, social theorist and philosopher. Among the over sixty books attributed to him, *Floor Games* is rarely ever listed. Despite its relative obscurity in Wells' diverse body of creative efforts, the little book of *Floor Games* inadvertently, but quite profoundly, impacted the future of child psychotherapy. In that light, we will take a look at the life of H.G. Wells, with particular focus on the development of the creative, playful aspects of his nature. We will also examine some of the complexities and conflicts in the life of the man who, in 1911, was motivated to pen the small, but influential, literary work called *Floor Games*.

Born September 21, 1866, the son of a ladies' maid and a gardener, Herbert George Wells' early life was spent in impoverished circumstances, both materially and intellectually. His mother and father ran a crockery shop in the front of their home, which sat on a small street in a poor, working class section of London.

Wells described his mother as *burdened with hardship* and *broken* following the sudden death of his sister, Fanny, two years before his birth. Struggling to survive on their meager

***Editor's Note:** We extend our grateful thanks to A.P. Watt, Ltd., on behalf of the Literary Executors of the Estate of H.G. Wells, for permission to include the photographs of Wells as a boy, Wells and Jane on their bicycle and the Wells children as infants, as well as the picshua illustration of daily life in the Wells household. All are from H.G. Wells' Experiment in Autobiography: Discoveries and Conclusions of a Very Ordinary Brain (Since 1866), copyright 1934 by H.G. Wells, published by The Macmillan Company, New York.*

H.G. Wells, c. 1876. (By permission of A.P. Watt Ltd. on behalf of the Literary Executors of the Estate of H.G. Wells.)

means, Mr. and Mrs. Wells' time was fully consumed with running the shop and maintaining their modest home. The grimy back yard was the only space available for Wells and his three brothers to wander. It was a confined 30- by 40-foot walled yard, sharing space with the necessities of the time — the outhouse, water well, and the incinerator. Additional stock for the crockery shop was also kept in this utilitarian area. Reflecting on his childhood in his autobiography, Wells described that little enclosure as, "...a large part of my world in those days" (p. 24).

With little adult encouragement or guidance, Wells found a place to play and had abundant unstructured time. Through his natural need for creative activity, Wells fashioned his props from the little that was available to him. Being poor and having no real toys, little *Bertie*, as he was known, made his own by forming the ashes and eggshells in the back yard incinerator into battle games and other fanciful landscapes. It is interesting that, like the sandplay it would eventually inspire, Wells' early play was with small toys on a sandy ground. Wells would later account for his battle play in another tiny volume, *Little Wars*, in which he describes the rules for his miniature war games. Never losing his love for play, Wells said he played these games regularly throughout his adult life.

Wells had a love for learning. At age seven, he suffered a broken leg, which confined him to bed for over a year. During this time he developed a vigorous appetite for reading. Poverty, tuberculosis and damaged kidneys conspired to limit his early schooling to age 13.

As a young man, Wells worked briefly as a clerk, and he also tried his hand as a pharmacy assistant. He determined himself generally unsuited to most labors, and he thus returned to education in the 1880s, where he found his niche as a student. An unfortunate financial hardship, however, forced him to leave school and work for two years in a tailor's shop. Albeit frustrating, this experience served to cement Wells' resolve to complete his education.

Wells possessed a deeply questioning mind. In his *Experiment in Autobiography*, written in 1934, he poignantly commented,

> *It seemed to me much more important to know whether or not I was immortal than whether or no I was to make a satisfactory shop assistant* (p. 126).

His arduous course of self-study in the sciences ultimately landed him a scholarship as a teacher in training under T.H. Huxley, an eminent professor. Wells earned a bachelor's degree in 1890.

Wells had a rocky marital life. In October 31, 1891 he married his cousin, Isabel. Wells' love for Isabel was deeply rooted in his early years. They had lived together in his aunt's home, growing through their adolescence like brother and sister. However, fundamental personality differences existed between Isabel and Wells. Isabel was grounded in a sound, conventional nature and outlook, while Wells was deeply concerned with the discrepancies between social conventions and the real life values underlying them. This, combined with his sensitive emotional temperament prone to irritability, exacted its toll on the relationship. By Wells' own admission, these tensions were fueled by his roving eye and enchantment with a bright student named Amy Catherine Robbins. Wells realized that, in spite of his profound love and respect for Isabel, their relationship was altogether untenable. Their marriage lasted until December 1893, a little more than two years. In early 1894, Wells scandalized 19th century Victorian England by leaving Isabel and moving in with Catherine, whom he called *Jane*. Wells and Jane married in 1895.

Wells described himself as sexually driven, resulting in his inability to develop a relationship that satisfactorily matched his expectations and fantasies. Wells thus began a series of affairs and dalliances. Later, in his more mature years, Wells would characterize this phase of his life as disordered and at split purposes with his highly valued pursuits.

For years, Wells remained intensely conflicted about leaving Isabel for Jane. With cultivated wisdom he came to recognize that he had projected the image of a goddess, first onto Isabel, then Jane, seeking in them a missing part of himself. Wells was extremely angry and jealous when Isabel remarried. Many years hence, however, he was able to overcome his fixation on Isabel, and their renewed friendship lasted until her death.

During Wells' early career as a teacher, he supplemented his scant income by writing miscellaneous articles. Ill health eventually forced him to abandon his teaching activities. Thereafter, he devoted his full time efforts toward writing. His years of financial struggle eased with his growing success. Wells was able to move his parents out of their cramped, unhealthy house to a much nicer home he eventually purchased for them.

Among his many creative activities, Wells made sketches and drawings to illustrate his frequent letters to friends and family. In 1893, he began drawing what he called *picshuas* (next page) for Jane and himself, illustrating events of their lives and relationship. A frequent theme in the picshuas was Jane reprimanding Wells with an umbrella for having committed a preposterous *faux pas*. A complex and conflicted man, Wells' generous sense of humor remained a big part of his life, softening the difficulties he would encounter with friends and family. A description of the picshuas in his and Jane's lives, excerpted from his autobiography, reveals Wells' remarkably playful humor and its integral role in his daily life.

> *...and when we were sitting together in the evening, with my writing things before me I would break off my work to do "picshuas," these silly little sketches about this or that incident which became at last a sort of burlesque diary of our lives and accumulated in boxes until there were hundreds of them. ...A burlesque description I gave, after a visit to the Zoological Gardens, of the high intelligence and remarkable social life of the gopher,*

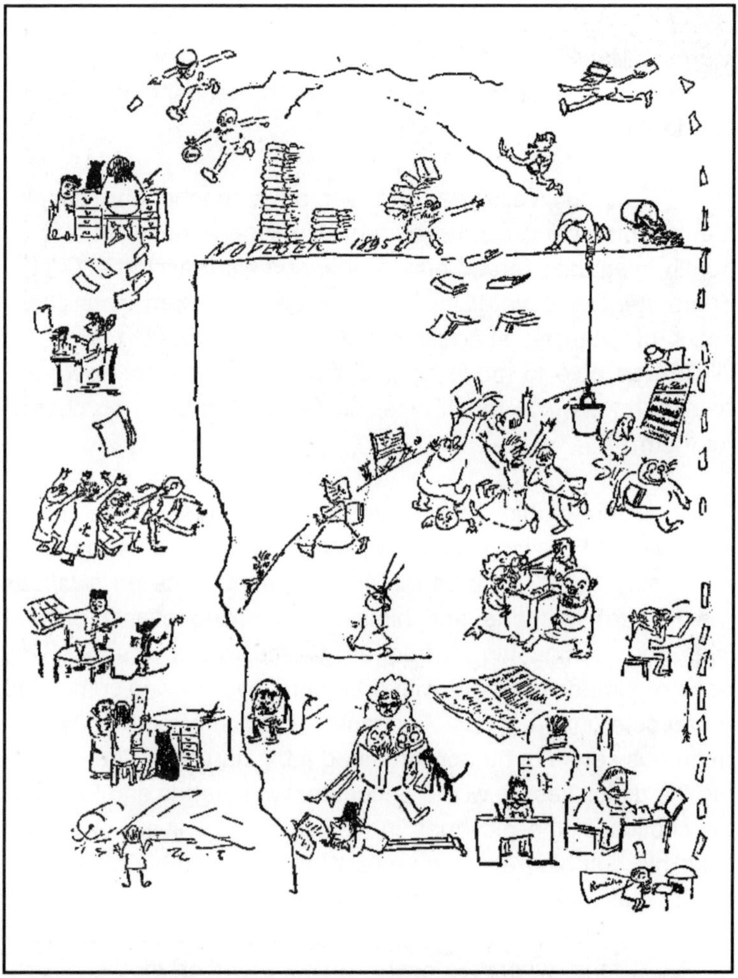

This picshua playfully documents the active daily life of Wells at home. Among other humorous activities he writes, runs back and forth to the post, reads a manuscript to the cat, works on his garden, is harangued by editors and reads a book with his sons. (By permission of A.P. Watt Ltd. on behalf of the Literary Executors of the Estate of H.G. Wells.)

amused us so much that we incorporated a sort of gopher chorus with the picshuas. Whatever we did, whatever was going on in the world, the gophers set about doing after their

H.G. Wells and Amy Catherine Wells, 1895. (By permission of A.P. Watt Ltd. on behalf of the Literary Executors of the Estate of H.G. Wells.)

> *fashion. Into this parallel world of burlesque and fancy, we transferred a very considerable amount of our every-day life, and there it lost its weight and irksomeness (pp.* 365-6).

Wells' love of play was woven throughout his life, as the photograph of H.G. and Jane illustrates. Due to Jane's bouts of ill health, Wells purchased a Humber tandem bicycle for exercise and fresh air. Sunny days would have H.G. and Jane pedaling about the southern English countryside, attracting astonished glances wherever they went.

By 1900, Jane and H.G. Wells began their family. They had two sons, G.P. "Gip" and Frank R. Wells, with whom Wells was to share his avid respect for creative play.

F.R. Wells and G.P. Wells, 1906. (By permission of A.P. Watt Ltd. on behalf of the Literary Executors of the Estate of H.G. Wells.)

Perhaps as a result of his early pleasures with play in the scant circumstances of his family, Wells retained a fervent belief in the creative, playful richness of life, as well as an open distaste for the demands of a capitalist society that compels acquisitiveness and acquiescence. Above all else, Wells respected the playful and artistic impulse.

In 1911, Wells wrote *Floor* Games, the joyful account of play with his sons in their magical worlds and kingdoms on the nursery floor. An announcement of the book appearing in *The Delineator* in January 1913 advises all grown ups to read the book, as it shows how to become better fathers, mothers, uncles and aunts.

Despite its playful charm, *Floor Games* had a limited life and quickly receded into literary history. Absent mainstream critical acclaim, the delightful spark of *Floor Games* nevertheless illumined an entire profession of healing work with children, through its influence on the psycho-

THE DELINEATOR FOR JANUARY 1913 PAGE 53

BOOKS FOR HOLIDAY GIFTS

By James Shelley Hamilton

The boy in H.G. Wells is writing about the games that he and the junior Wellses play. They are fascinating games, with inexhaustible possibilities – the kind that give the greatest joy because they keep the imagination and the hands busy at the same time, creating. Every grown-up should read this book, because it points out a quite definite way to become better fathers, mothers, uncles, and aunts.

Floor Games, by H.G. Wells. (Small, Maynard & Co.) $1.00.

Newspaper promotion of Wells' *Floor Games*. *The Delineator*, January 1913.

therapeutic methods of British pediatrician, Dr. Margaret Lowenfeld and Swiss Jungian therapist, Dora Maria Kalff. We will examine the nature of this influence in the next chapters.

Wells' prolific writing career continued throughout his lifetime. During the last 20 years of his life, Wells produced over 40 books. H.G. Wells died in London on August 13, 1946.

Margaret Lowenfeld

Founder of the World Technique

Dr. Margaret Lowenfeld was a pioneer in the psychotherapeutic treatment of children. Following World War I, Lowenfeld, a young British pediatrician, returned to Poland, her ancestral home, to work with victims of the Russian-Polish war. Her direct experiences of horror and the devastation of war on children evoked a profound urgency to help alleviate their suffering. Acting upon her deep motivation, Lowenfeld established one of the first psychotherapeutic treatment centers for children in London in the autumn of 1928. First called the *Clinic for Nervous and Difficult Children*, it was later named the *Institute for Child Psychology*.

Lowenfeld understood children well, realizing that their thought processes are complex and frequently occur simultaneously on many levels. Early in her work she recognized that attempting to address the psychological suffering of children with words was a hopeless endeavor. She understood the developmental nature of children's growing cognitive capacities and saw the futility of expecting them to employ the more advanced skills required to analyze or talk about their inner worlds. Dr. Lowenfeld knew that the tool she sought for her work with children must encompass the whole field of the child's inner experience, and that it must be non-verbal. Lowenfeld needed a method that would allow a clinician to directly record the child's inner experience — one that was as free of adult interference as possible. Lowenfeld theorized that communication of any depth and therapeutic significance with children would occur through their natural language of play.

Lowenfeld's urgent desire to provide direct and appropriate psychological help to children collided with her clear understanding of the developmental differences and limitations of young minds. As the human creative process often works, the seeming incompatibility of these oppositional forces ignited a spark of memory in Dr. Lowenfeld, whereupon she recalled reading *Floor Games,* the tiny and little-known volume written by eminent writer H.G. Wells, chronicling the play of his two sons. Through reading *Floor Games*, Dr. Lowenfeld recognized that with toys, a place to play, and appropriate adult interaction, the Wells boys were free to play out their inner worlds. Lowenfeld saw that by creating their own miniature worlds, the children directly communicated their inner experiences and explored new ways of being and thinking.

With the miniature worlds of *Floor Games* in mind, Dr. Lowenfeld assembled what the children in her clinic came to call the *wonder box*. In it she gathered a wide variety of small materials such as beads, match boxes and colored sticks. The box grew to include miniature animals, people, houses and other elements of the children's lives and was soon called the *world*. The children instinctively assembled figures from the world collection in the tray of sand, and thus Lowenfeld's *World Technique* was born.

Lowenfeld's theories evolved completely out of her work with the children; they were not superimposed. She greatly appreciated the singularity of each individual's healing experience, understanding that rather than conforming to externally imposed theories, healing arises from the combined forces of background and temperament. Lowenfeld observed that therapeutic change occurs through the images in the sand tray in ways that make sense to each child. In all instances, she let the children's work guide her understanding of their psychological pain and healing processes.

Lowenfeld introduced the method in her clinic by engaging each child in a brief discussion about how children frequently think in pictures, which better describe their worlds than do words. Following an introduction to the tray of sand and the available toys and materials, Lowenfeld simply invited the child to "...make whatever comes into his (or her) head."

The first record of a sand tray was documented at the clinic in 1929. Since that time, the World Technique has proliferated around the globe and is now used for both child and adult treatment. As a non-verbal tool, the World Technique is effective across cultures, permitting healing and deepened self-understanding irrespective of background and circumstances.

Dr. Lowenfeld died in 1973. Her valuable work lives on through the teachings of the Dr. Margaret Lowenfeld Trust (in conjunction with Middlesex University in England), through practitioners of the World Technique as a therapeutic modality, and as a result of Lowenfeld's influence on the future of therapeutic techniques involving *play*. In the next section, we will examine the way in which Lowenfeld's World Technique gave rise to Dora Maria Kalff's therapeutic method known as *sandplay*.

Dora Maria Kalff

Pioneer of the Sandplay Method

Like Margaret Lowenfeld, Dora Maria Kalff of Switzerland undertook the study of psychology following the hardships of war. Kalff's mentors, Carl Gustav Jung and Emma Jung, recognized her natural abilities with children and encouraged her to pursue child treatment. This launched Kalff's quest for a way to use the analytical tools of Jung, (generally undertaken with dream work and verbal analysis), with the less cognitively developed minds of children.

Dora Kalff with child at sand tray.

In 1954, at a congress in Zurich, Kalff attended a presentation of the World Technique by Dr. Margaret Lowenfeld. Greatly impressed with Lowenfeld's profound understanding of the language of children, Kalff undertook a year-long course of study with Lowenfeld at the Institute for Child Psychology in London.

As Kalff gained clinical experience in child therapy, she began to recognize patterns in the communications of the children in their sand tray worlds. Kalff soon noticed that what was occurring in the images in the sand was the *individuation* process described by Jung. Kalff saw that by holding this awareness and refraining from interpretation, a profound process of psychic re-ordering was set in motion. Kalff observed that, over the course of a series of sand tray creations, the individuation process occurs symbolically and non-verbally in the context of

Dora Kalff teaching a sandplay therapy class in 1988.

play, which is perfectly suited to children. Kalff shared her observations with Margaret Lowenfeld, and they mutually acknowledged the differences in their approaches. Both agreed that Kalff's method would be distinguished from the World Technique by the name of *sandplay*. (Additional details about Kalff's *Sandplay Method* will be discussed in the next section.)

Kalff was a founding member of the International Society for Sandplay Therapy. In addition to her clinical practice, she traveled extensively, conducting lectures and classes for sandplay therapists throughout the world. Kalff's only published work, *Sandplay: A Psychotherapeutic Approach to the Psyche*, was first released in the German language in 1979, and was translated into English in 1980.* Kalff's book has become a seminal classic work in the field of sandplay therapy.

Dora Maria Kalff continued her sandplay practice and teachings until shortly before her death in 1990.

Editor's Note: A new English language edition of Sandplay, A Psychotherapeutic Approach to the Psyche was released by Temenos Press in 2003. ISBN 0-9728517-0-4.

The Sandplay Method

The sandplay method consists of the psychotherapy client's creation of a three-dimensional picture, using miniature figures in a tray of sand, in the protective presence of the trained practitioner. The sand tray is 28-1/2 inches long by 19-1/2 inches wide and 3 inches deep. The sides and bottom of the inside of the sand tray are light blue.

By moving the sand aside, the blue coloration can be used to represent areas of water in the sandy landscape. Real water can be added to the sand to make it adaptable to shaping and sculpting. Miniature figures representing all aspects of life and fantasy are arranged on shelves near the sand tray, for convenient use by the client. In addition, a wide variety of building materials is available, out of which the client can fash-

Sand tray and collection of miniature figures.

ion needed items.

The client is encouraged by the therapist to make whatever he or she likes in the sand tray and is given no further instructions. As the client works in the sand tray, the therapist sits nearby making notes of the figures the client uses and what the client says, if anything. The therapist sketches a diagram of the sand tray for future reference and takes photos of the sand tray when completed. A sand tray picture is dismantled by the therapist, but not until the client has departed the session.

The theoretical foundation of sandplay therapy is based on the Jungian concept that the psyche has an autonomous disposition to heal, and that given the proper conditions, this natural tendency is activated. This is the individuation process that Dora Kalff first recognized in sandplay. Creating a series of three-dimensional sand trays facilitates healing and transformation by bringing up conflicts from the unconscious in symbolic form and allowing a healthy reordering of psychological contents.

Within the safety of the therapeutic relationship between therapist and client, sandplay allows the client to go beyond the limits of the conscious mind, to stimulate psychic development and to access channels to fuller, more creative living. No analysis or interpretation is made to the client until after the process is completed and sufficient time has passed to allow for the integration of the therapeutic work.

Although no interpretation is made with the client at the time of the production of the sand tray, it is very important that the therapist develop an understanding of what is transpiring in the client's transformative process. The therapist's understanding of the client's sandplay process plays a critical role in the "containment," or "holding," of the client's emerging unconscious material. The therapist's more conscious awareness of the symbolic process, which is yet largely unconscious to the client, acts as a stabilizing factor to the often uncertain and tumultuous qualities of the emergence and integration of unconscious material for the client.

The therapist's capacity to contain the client's emerging unconscious content works cooperatively with the client's ability to integrate and make conscious this symbolic material. In order to provide adequate containment, Dora Kalff advised that the sandplay therapist continually remain focused on and conscious of what is transpiring during the client's process, and continually refine his/her ability to analyze symbolic content. It is not necessary, nor possible, to understand everything that transpires in a sandplay process, as the nature of symbolic process is that it always leads beyond itself and is not reductive.

As with the World Technique, sandplay therapy is now used with adults and children. Jungian sandplay therapy is applied in a wide variety of clinical settings, and it is used for treatment of psychiatric disorders, developmental deprivation, trauma, and personal growth.

Today the teaching of sandplay therapy is carried on by the International Society for Sandplay Therapy and its affiliates in countries around the world. While sandplay therapy appears to be quite simple, it is a highly complex therapeutic modality and has profound potential. Qualified sandplay therapists undergo extensive training, personal process, and supervision in preparation for practice.

Web Resources

Topic	Resource and URL
H.G. Wells in the United Kingdom	**The H.G. Wells Society** www.personal.rdg.ac.uk/~lhsjamse/wells/wells.htm
H.G. Wells in the United States	**The H.G. Wells Society of the Americas** www.hgwellsusa.50megs.com
World Technique and Jungian Sandplay Therapy	**The Dr. Margaret Lowenfeld Trust** http://www.lowenfeld.org/ **The Sandplay Therapists of America** www.sandplay.org
Play therapy in the United Kingdom	**The British Association of Play Therapists** www.bapt.info
Play therapy in the United States	**The Association for Play Therapy** www.a4pt.org
Books on sandplay therapy	**Temenos Press** www.temenospress.com

Conclusion

H.G. Wells loved play and celebrated its necessary role in imaginative living. His prolifically creative life is a testament to the aptness of his respect for play. *Floor Games* invites us into the magical realms beyond the doors of the Wells' nursery, and its magic continues to live on in ways Wells may never have imagined. Combined with the insight and wisdom of early child treatment pioneers Margaret Lowenfeld and Dora Kalff, *Floor Games* inspired the fields of play therapy and sandplay therapy. These treatment modalities continue to relieve suffering, promote healing, and restore hope to thousands of children and adults around the world.

Thank you, Mr. Wells. Through *Floor Games*, you have profoundly influenced psychotherapeutic methods, and you have thoughtfully etched an indelible reminder upon all of us that, regardless of age or circumstance, play is an essential component of life.

It is my hope that the joyful, playful spirit of H.G. Wells will continue to inspire the spirit of play in parents, teachers, healers, and grown-ups of all sorts, whose good fortune happens upon this enchanting tale of the worlds the Wells children created on their nursery floor. Our children need this delight, and our world is hungry for it.

Barbara A. Turner, Ph.D.
Editor

About the Editor

Barbara A. Turner is a sandplay therapist and teacher. She began her studies of sandplay therapy with Dora M. Kalff in Switzerland and is the editor and author of a number of classic books in the field. Among them are Dora M. Kalff's *Sandplay: A Psychotherapeutic Approach to the Psyche* and Estelle L. Weinrib's *Images of the Self: The Sandplay Therapy Process.*

Dr. Turner is the author of *The Handbook of Sandplay Therapy.* She lives and works in Northern California.

Reader's Notes

Reader's Notes